GRADE K

Reader's and Writer's JOURNAL

PEARSON

Glenview, Illinois • Boston, Massachusetts • Chandler, Arizona • Hoboken, New Jersey

ISBN-13: 978-0-328-78880-4
ISBN-10: 0-328-78880-5
2 3 4 5 6 7 8 9 10 V004 18 17 16 15 14

Table of Contents

Unit 1 Living Together: This Is Home

Module A

Module B

Unit 2 Understanding Then and Now

Module A

Module B

Unit 3 Predicting Change

Unit 4 Learning About Each Other and the World

Unit 5 Knowing About Patterns and Structures

Unit 6 Exploring Communities

Name ______________________________

Explore the Text

● Lesson 1

■ Lesson 2

▲ Lesson 3

Children ask and answer questions about text to demonstrate comprehension.

Name ______________________________

Explore the Text

Lesson 4

Lesson 5

Children ask and answer questions about text to demonstrate comprehension.

Name ______________________

Benchmark Vocabulary

● **Lesson 1** island, ducks

■ **Lesson 2** peanuts, waddled

▲ **Lesson 3** flapped

Children demonstrate contextual understanding of Benchmark Vocabulary.

Name ________________________________

Benchmark Vocabulary

Lesson 4 build, cozy

Lesson 5 quacked

Children demonstrate contextual understanding of Benchmark Vocabulary.

Name ______________________

Write the words on the lines.

● **Lesson 1**

cab

■ **Lesson 2**

fed

▲ **Lesson 3**

bag

hid

Children practice various conventions of standard English.

Name ______________________________

Write the words on the lines.

Lesson 4

kid

leg

Lesson 5

jam

nod

Children practice various conventions of standard English.

Name ______________________________

● Lesson 1 Draw a picture.

■ Lesson 2 Draw a picture. Write about it.

▲ Lesson 3 Draw a picture.

Children read text closely and use text evidence in their written answers.

Name ______________________________

Writing in Response to Reading

■ Lesson 4 Draw a picture. Write about it.

◆ Lesson 5 Write about a place.

Children read text closely and use text evidence in their written answers.

Is Tab in the bin?

I look in the bin.

See tab!

She naps in the bin.

Looking for Tab

I am sad.

My cat Tab ran.

Name ______________________

Is Tab on the mat?

I look at the mat.

No Tab.

Is Tab in the cot?

I look at the cot.

No Tab.

Name ______________________

Name ________________________________

Explore the Text

Lesson 6

Lesson 7

Lesson 8

Children ask and answer questions about text to demonstrate comprehension.

Name ______________________________

Explore the Text

♥ Lesson 9

✱ Lesson 10

Children ask and answer questions about text to demonstrate comprehension.

Name ______________________________

Lesson 6 satisfied, waded

Lesson 7 tumbled, marching

Lesson 8 beckoned, rushed

Children demonstrate contextual understanding of Benchmark Vocabulary.

Name ______________________________

Benchmark Vocabulary

♥ **Lesson 9** snug, frightening, wiggling, waggling

✱ **Lesson 10** swayed, flock, prickly, fierce

Children demonstrate contextual understanding of Benchmark Vocabulary.

Name

Conventions

Write the words on the lines.

Lesson 6

rap

Lesson 7

sit

quit

Lesson 8

wax

vet

Children practice various conventions of standard English.

Name ______________________

Conventions

Write the words on the lines.

Lesson 9

yam

zip

✱ Lesson 10

slip

crab

snug

Children practice various conventions of standard English.

Name ______________________________

Lesson 6 Draw a picture. Write about it.

Lesson 7 Write your opinion.

Lesson 8 Write your response.

Children read text closely and use text evidence in their written answers.

Name ______________________

Lesson 9 Write a detail.

Lesson 10 Write the order.

Children read text closely and use text evidence in their written answers.

Kim, we can get the cat.

Kip, we can get the rat.

Let's Get a Pet

I am Kim.

I am Kip.

We look for a pet.

Name ______________________________

See the tan cat, Kim.

We can get it.

See the little rat, Kip.

We can get it.

Name ______________________

Name ______________________________

Explore the Text

Lesson 11

Lesson 12

Children ask and answer questions about text to demonstrate comprehension.

Name ___________________________

Explore the Text

Lesson 13

Children ask and answer questions about text to demonstrate comprehension.

Name ______________________________

Benchmark Vocabulary

Lesson 11 grazed, darting

Lesson 12 build, frightening

Children demonstrate contextual understanding of Benchmark Vocabulary.

Name ____

Benchmark Vocabulary

Lesson 13 waded, grazed

Children demonstrate contextual understanding of Benchmark Vocabulary.

Name ______________________________

Conventions

Write the sentence. Use a capital letter.

Lesson 11

we can run. ______________________________

the dog barks. ______________________________

he is fast. ______________________________

Write your own sentence. Use a capital letter.

____

____

Children practice various conventions of standard English.

Name ______________________

Conventions

Lesson 12 Write the sentence. Add the end punctuation.

Can you go ______________________

Look out ______________________

Lesson 13 Write *I* on the line.

______________ like blue.

Write a sentence with the word *I*.

____

Children practice various conventions of standard English.

Name ______________________________

Lesson 11 Write your opinion.

Lesson 12 Write your opinion.

Lesson 13 Write your response.

Children read text closely and use text evidence in their written answers.

Name ________________________________

Lesson 12 Draw a picture. Write a detail about it.

Children write routinely for a range of tasks, purposes, and audiences.

Get the top, Mom!

Mom gets the top.

The top is on the pan.

POP! POP!

Look at the pot.

The pot is hot.

Name ______________________________

Pop! Pop!

Get the top, Dad!

Dad gets the top.

The top is on the pot.

Look at the pan.

The pan is hot.

Pop! Pop!

Name ______________________

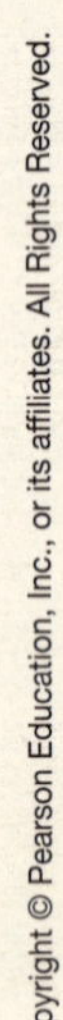

Name ____________________

Explore the Text

● Lesson 1

■ Lesson 2

▲ Lesson 3

Children ask and answer questions about text to demonstrate comprehension.

Name ______________________________

Explore the Text

Lesson 4

Lesson 5

Children ask and answer questions about text to demonstrate comprehension.

Name ______________________________

Lesson 1 pond, shallow

Lesson 2 lakes, forests, farms

Children demonstrate contextual understanding of Benchmark Vocabulary.

Name ______________________

Benchmark Vocabulary

Lesson 3 dive, underwater

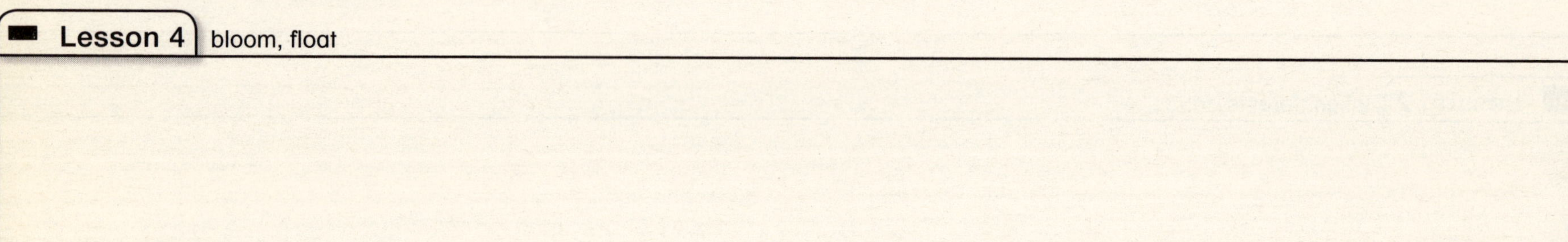

Lesson 4 bloom, float

Lesson 5 together

Children demonstrate contextual understanding of Benchmark Vocabulary.

Name ______________________________

● Lesson 1

Draw an X on the noun that names an animal. Say the word.

dog

book

■ ▲ Lesson 2 and 3

Circle the noun that names a place. Draw an X on the noun that names a thing.

bus

park

Children practice various conventions of standard English.

Name ______________________________

Lesson 4

Circle the noun that names a person. Say the word.

house

boy

◆ Lesson 5

Draw an X on the noun that names more than one. Say the word.

hats

flower

Children practice various conventions of standard English.

Name ______________________________

● Lesson 1 Draw your picture on a separate sheet of paper. Write about it.

■ Lesson 2 Draw a picture on a separate sheet of paper. Write about it.

▲ Lesson 3 Write one detail.

Children read text closely and use text evidence in their written answers.

Name

Writing in Response to Reading

Lesson 4 Write your opinion.

Lesson 5 Write your response.

Children read text closely and use text evidence in their written answers.

Pam and I sit.

We have to rest!

I look at Pam.

I rap.

Look At Me

Pam looks at me.

I tap.

Pam taps like me.

Name ______________________

I nod.

Pam nods like me.

I look at Pam.

Pam pats.

I pat like Pam.

Pam hops.

I hop like Pam.

Name ______________________________

Name ________________________________

Explore the Text

Lesson 6

Lesson 7

Lesson 8

Children ask and answer questions about text to demonstrate comprehension.

Name ______________________________

Explore the Text

♥ Lesson 9

✱ Lesson 10

Children ask and answer questions about text to demonstrate comprehension.

Name ____________________

Benchmark Vocabulary

Lesson 6 full

Lesson 7 gathers, scurries

Lesson 8 rotten, trembles

Children demonstrate contextual understanding of Benchmark Vocabulary.

Name ____________________

Benchmark Vocabulary

Lesson 9 cling, huddle, damp, frozen

Lesson 10 swoops, meadow, nest, cave

Children demonstrate contextual understanding of Benchmark Vocabulary.

Name ____________________

Lesson 6 Draw a noun that names more than one.

Lesson 7 Draw a picture of what you can do. Label it.

Children practice various conventions of standard English.

Name ______________________________

Conventions

Lessons 8 and 9 Draw a picture for one question. Write a question word.

Lesson 10 Write your sentence.

Children practice various conventions of standard English.

Name ______________________________

Lesson 6 Write your opinion.

Lesson 7 Write *yes* or *no*.

Draw a picture on a separate sheet of paper to support your opinion.

Lesson 8 Draw the animal's winter home.

Children read text closely and use text evidence in their written answers.

Name ______________________

Writing in Response to Reading

♥ Lesson 9 Draw your answer.

✱ Lesson 10 Write the meanings of the words.

Children read text closely and use text evidence in their written answers.

Look, Sam.

It is a mat for you.

Sam likes *my* mat.

Mim's Cat Sam

I am Mim.

I have a cat.

My cat is Sam.

Name ______________________________

I sit on my mat.

Sam sits on me.

I nap on my mat.

Sam naps on me.

Sam is not little.

Sam is BIG.

Name ______________________

Name ____________________________________

Lesson 11

Children ask and answer questions about text to demonstrate comprehensio.

Name ______________________________

Explore the Text

Lesson 12

Children ask and answer questions about text to demonstrate comprehension.

Name ____________________

Benchmark Vocabulary

Lesson 11 shallow, trembles

Children demonstrate contextual understanding of Benchmark Vocabulary.

Name ______________________________

Benchmark Vocabulary

Lesson 12 together, gathers

Children demonstrate contextual understanding of Benchmark Vocabulary.

Name ______________________

Lesson 11 Listen to the words. Write the words on the lines.

Children practice various conventions of standard English.

Name ______________________

Lesson 12 Listen to the words. Write the words on the lines.

Children practice various conventions of standard English.

Name ____________________

Lesson 11 Write your opinion.

Lesson 12 Write your response.

Children read text closely and use text evidence in their written answers.

Name

Lesson 12 Draw a picture. Label your drawing.

Write about your picture.

Children write routinely for a range of tasks, purposes, and audiences.

Look at Dot and Ted.

Dot can pat Tim.

Ted can pat Tim.

They like Tim the pig!

Can We Pat Tim?

Tim is a pig.

He is not a little pig.

Name ______________________________

Dot and Ted look at Tim.

A pig is not a cat.

A pig is not a dog.

You can pat a cat.

You can pat a dog.

Can you pat a pig?

Name ______________________________

Name ______________________________

Explore the Text

Lesson 1

Lesson 2

Lesson 3

Children ask and answer questions about text to demonstrate comprehension.

Name ______________________________

Explore the Text

■ Lesson 4

◆ Lesson 5

Children ask and answer questions about text to demonstrate comprehension.

Name ______________________

Benchmark Vocabulary

● **Lesson 1** country, curious

■ **Lesson 2** spring, droops

▲ **Lesson 3** buds, swell, brook

Children demonstrate contextual understanding of Benchmark Vocabulary.

Name ______________________________

Benchmark Vocabulary

Lesson 4 carriage, cellars, stories

Lesson 5 shabby, shutters

Children demonstrate contextual understanding of Benchmark Vocabulary.

Name ______________________________

● Lesson 1 Name the pictures. Circle the verb and color the picture.

dig

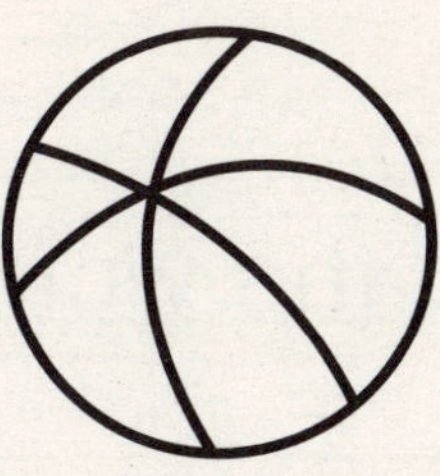

ball

■ Lesson 2 Name the pictures. Circle the verb and color the picture.

book

read

Children practice various conventions of standard English.

Name ______________________

▲ Lesson 3 Circle the verbs.

run tree sit cat

▬ Lesson 4 Listen to the words. Spell the words.

◆ Lesson 5 Write a sentence.

Children practice various conventions of standard English.

Name ____________________

● Lesson 1 Write a detail about how the setting changes.

■ Lesson 2 Write about what the words and illustrations tell you.

▲ Lesson 3 Draw a picture of the words. Label them.

Children read text closely and use text evidence in their written answers.

Name

Writing in Response to Reading

Lesson 4 Write your opinion.

Lesson 5 Draw two pictures. Label them.

Children practice various conventions of standard English.

Stop the fan, Pam!

Pam and Dan

Pam the ant has a fan.

She is hot, hot, hot!

Name ____________________

Pam will fan and fan.

Pam can fan fast!

The fan is bad for Dan.

Dan has no cap!

Dan has no bag!

Dan has no mat!

Name ___________________________

Name ____________________

Lesson 6

Lesson 7

Lesson 8

Children ask and answer questions about text to demonstrate comprehension.

Name ____________________

Explore the Text

♥ Lesson 9

✱ Lesson 10

Children ask and answer questions about text to demonstrate comprehension.

Name ______________________________

Benchmark Vocabulary

Lesson 6 plow

Lesson 7 flutter, sprouts, bouquets

Lesson 8 shrivel up, ripe, frantically

Children demonstrate contextual understanding of Benchmark Vocabulary.

Name ______________________________

Benchmark Vocabulary

Lesson 9 crackle, twirling, slippery, peck

Lesson 10 frost, harvest

Children demonstrate contextual understanding of Benchmark Vocabulary.

Name ______________________

Lesson 6 Write a sentence.

Lesson 7 Write an end punctuation mark.

Watch the plants grow

The girl plants a seed

Lesson 8 Listen to the words. Spell the words.

Children practice various conventions of standard English.

Name ______________________

Lesson 9 Write a question.

Lesson 10 Write an end punctuation mark.

Where is she going

What will we do in the city

Children practice various conventions of standard English.

Name ______________________________

Lesson 6 Draw a picture. Write a sentence.

Lesson 7 Draw a picture. Write a question.

Children read text closely and use text evidence in their written answers.

Name ______________________

Lesson 8 Draw your picture on a separate sheet of paper. Write a label.

Lesson 9 Draw your picture on a separate sheet of paper. Write a caption.

Lesson 10 Write your opinion.

Children read text closely and use text evidence in their written answers.

Sal and Sid like little and big.

Little and Big

Sal and Sid like little.

They have a little cap.

They have a little top.

Name ______________________

Sid and Sal like big.

They have a big mat.

They have a big fan.

They do not have a big dog.

Can Sal and Sid get one?

Name ______________________

Name ________________________________

Explore the Text

Lesson 11

Lesson 12

Children ask and answer questions about text to demonstrate comprehension.

Name ______________________________

Explore the Text

Lesson 13

Children ask and answer questions about text to demonstrate comprehension.

Name ______________________________

Benchmark Vocabulary

Lesson 11 gasoline, glance, twinkled

Lesson 12 curious, shabby, sprouts, droops

Children demonstrate contextual understanding of Benchmark Vocabulary.

Name ______________________________

Benchmark Vocabulary

☀ **Lesson 13** harvest, glance, ripe, slippery

Children demonstrate contextual understanding of Benchmark Vocabulary.

Name ______________________

Lesson 11 Circle the complete sentence.

1. My chair

   Look at that bug!

2. I hope it is red!

   red car

Write a sentence.

____

____

Children practice various conventions of standard English.

Name ______________________

Lesson 12 Write an end punctuation mark.

Be careful ______ This is fun ______

Write the sentence. Add the end punctuation.

That girl is fast

Lesson 13 Listen to the words. Spell the words.

Children practice various conventions of standard English.

Name ______________________

Lesson 11 Write your response.

Lesson 12 Write your response.

Lesson 13 Write your opinion.

Children read text closely and use text evidence in their written answers.

Name ______________________

Writing

✱ Lesson 10 Draw a picture that shows the season you like best. Write to tell why.

Children write routinely for a range of tasks, purposes, and audiences.

Peg and Pam pat
the pigs.

Pigs are the best pets.

Big Pal and Little Pip

Peg has a pet pig.

It is a big pig.

Name ______________________________

The big pig is Pal.

Pal is in the pen.

Here is a pan, Pal.

Pam has a pet pig.

It is a little pig.

The little pig is Pip.

Pip is in the pen.

Name ______________________________

Name ______________________________

● Lesson 1

■ Lesson 2

▲ Lesson 3

Children ask and answer questions about text to demonstrate comprehension.

Name ______________________________

Explore the Text

Lesson 4

Lesson 5

Children ask and answer questions about text to demonstrate comprehension.

Name ____________________

Benchmark Vocabulary

Lesson 1 century, graze

Lesson 2 proudly

Children demonstrate contextual understanding of Benchmark Vocabulary.

Name ______________________________

Benchmark Vocabulary

▲ **Lesson 3** dozen, ample

▬ **Lesson 4** heaps, haul

◆ **Lesson 5** descended, breezy

Children demonstrate contextual understanding of Benchmark Vocabulary.

Name ____________________

● Lesson 1

The cat sleeps and ____________________.

■ Lesson 2

The dog and ____________________ play.

▲ Lesson 3 Listen to the words. Write the words on the lines.

Children practice various conventions of standard English.

Name ______________________

Lesson 4 Add a detail.

I like the bike.

I like the ______________________ bike.

Lesson 5 Add a detail.

The cat jumps.

The ______________________

cat jumps.

Children practice various conventions of standard English.

Name ______________________________

● Lesson 1 Draw a picture. Write about it.

■ Lesson 2 Write your response.

▲ Lesson 3 Write your question.

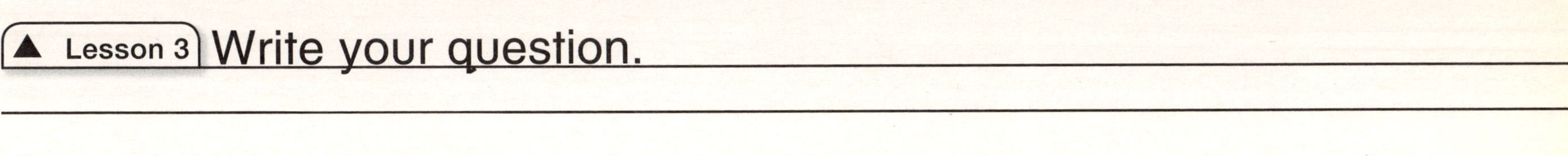

Children read text closely and use text evidence in their written answers.

Name ______________________

Writing in Response to Reading

Lesson 4 Write your response.

Lesson 5 Write your answer.

Children read text closely and use text evidence in their written answers.

Can the cat sit and sip?
Here is milk for the cat.
The cat can sit and sip.

We Can Sit and Sip

Cam can sit.
Cam can sip.
Cam can sip from the cup.

Name ______________________________

Ric can sit and sip.
Get Ric a cup.
Ric can sip from the cup.

I have a cup.
I can sit with Cam and Ric.
I can sip with Ric and Cam.

Name ______________________

Name ________________________________

Explore the Text

Lesson 6

Lesson 7

Lesson 8

Children ask and answer questions about text to demonstrate comprehension.

Name ______________________

Explore the Text

♥ Lesson 9

✱ Lesson 10

Children ask and answer questions about text to demonstrate comprehension.

Name ______________________________

Benchmark Vocabulary

Lesson 6 nibbled, paddle, canoe, generation

Lesson 7 tradition

Lesson 8 creaky, clanking

Children demonstrate contextual understanding of Benchmark Vocabulary.

Name ______________________

Benchmark Vocabulary

♥ **Lesson 9** caves, fireplace

✱ **Lesson 10** well, faucet

Children demonstrate contextual understanding of Benchmark Vocabulary.

Name ______________________

Conventions

Lesson 6 Listen to the words. Write the words on the lines.

Lesson 7 Circle the prepositions. Write a sentence.

The bird flew out the window. Tim is in his room.

Children practice various conventions of standard English.

Name ___________________________

Lesson 8 Circle the prepositions.

I go to school.

I got a letter from my friend.

Lesson 9 Circle the prepositions.

The bird hops off the bush.

The plates are on the table.

Lesson 10 Circle the prepositions.

I walk by the library.

I play baseball for fun.

Children practice various conventions of standard English.

Name ________________________________

Lesson 6 Write your response.

Lesson 7 Write a detail.

Lesson 8 Draw a picture. Label it.

Children read text closely and use text evidence in their written answers.

Writing in Response to Reading

Name ____________________

♥ Lesson 9 Draw a picture. Label it.

✱ Lesson 10 Write your opinion.

Children read text closely and use text evidence in their written answers.

I will sit with Sid.

I look at Sid and grin.

I like Sid in the bin.

Sid in the Bin

Look at the bin.

The bin is not big.

The bin is little.

Name ______________________

Look at my dog Sid.
Sid is not big.
Sid is little.

He can fit in the bin.
Sit in the bin, Sid.
Sid is in the bin.

Name ___________________________

Name ________________________________

Explore the Text

Lesson 11

Children ask and answer questions about text to demonstrate comprehension.

Name ______________________________

Explore the Text

Lesson 12

Children ask and answer questions about text to demonstrate comprehension.

Name ______________________________

Benchmark Vocabulary

Lesson 11 century, dozen, caves, fireplace

Children demonstrate contextual understanding of Benchmark Vocabulary.

Name ______________________________

Benchmark Vocabulary

Lesson 12 heaps, breezy, well, faucet

Children demonstrate contextual understanding of Benchmark Vocabulary.

Name ______________________________

Lesson 11 Circle the prepositions. Write a sentence.

I live in a house of bricks.

Ben reads with his sister.

Children practice various conventions of standard English.

Name ______________________

Lesson 12 Listen to the words. Write the words on the lines.

Children practice various conventions of standard English.

Name ______________________

Lesson 11 Write your response.

Lesson 12 Write your response. Draw a picture on a separate sheet of paper.

Children read text closely and use text evidence in their written answers.

Name ______________________________

Writing

Lesson 12 Name the topic. Write your opinion.

Children write routinely for a range of tasks, purposes, and audiences.

They have a big fan.

It will fit in the big box.

Help me fit the fan in the box.

Will It Fit?

I have a pot.

Will it fit in the bag?

Name ______________________

The pot is little.
The bag is big.
The pot will fit in the bag.

We have a mop.
Will it fit in the bag?
It will fit in the big bag.

Name ______________________________

Name ______________________________

Explore the Text

● Lesson 1

■ Lesson 2

▲ Lesson 3

Children ask and answer questions about text to demonstrate comprehension.

Name ______________________

Explore the Text

Lesson 4

Lesson 5

Children ask and answer questions about text to demonstrate comprehension.

Name ______________________________

Benchmark Vocabulary

Lesson 1 squinting, glistening, soothed

Lesson 2 sighs, parched, rumbles

Children demonstrate contextual understanding of Benchmark Vocabulary.

Name ______________________________

Benchmark Vocabulary

▲ **Lesson 3** smartly, murmurs

■ **Lesson 4** swollen, plop, glazes, streaming

◆ **Lesson 5** racket, wordless, sparkles

Children demonstrate contextual understanding of Benchmark Vocabulary.

Name ______________________

● **Lesson 1** Listen to the words. Write the words.

■ **Lesson 2** Write one of the sentences.

▲ **Lesson 3** Write your name. Write your friend's name.

Children practice various conventions of standard English.

Name ______________________

Lesson 4 Write the sentence. Circle the uppercase letter.

Lesson 5 Write the sentence. Write your own sentence.

Children practice various conventions of standard English.

Name ______________________________

● Lesson 1 Draw a picture. Write about it.

■ Lesson 2 Write about the people or the weather.

▲ Lesson 3 Write the answer to the question.

Children read text closely and use text evidence in their written answers.

Name

Writing in Response to Reading

■ Lesson 4 Write the answer to the question.

◆ Lesson 5 Write your opinion. Write details that support it.

Children read text closely and use text evidence in their written answers.

I am Buzz the big bug.

My six legs let me run FAST.

Buzz

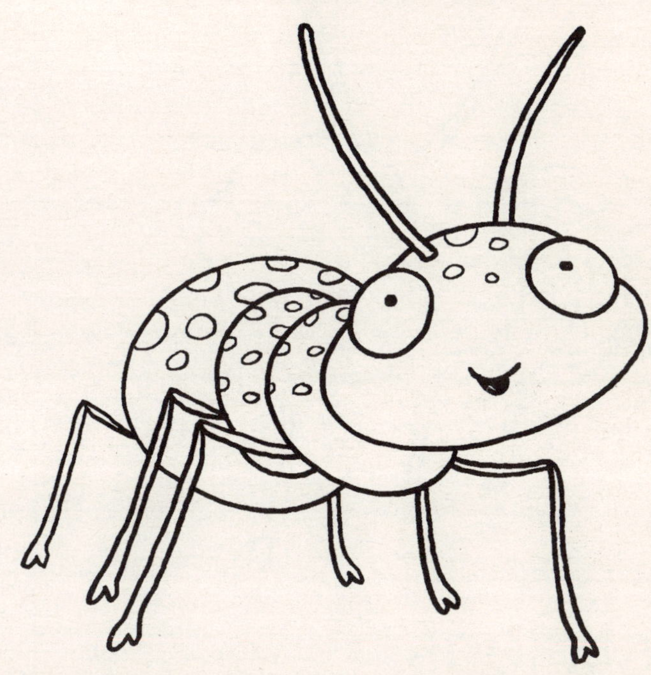

I am Buzz.

I am a big bug.

Name ______________________

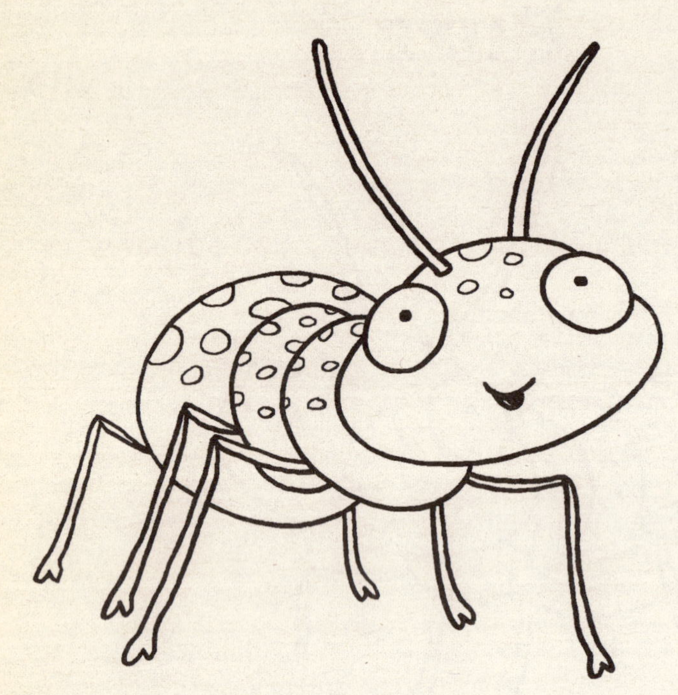

I have six legs.

I can run fast.

You can see me run.

You do not have six legs.

You have two legs.

You can run fast.

But not as fast as I can!

Name ____________________

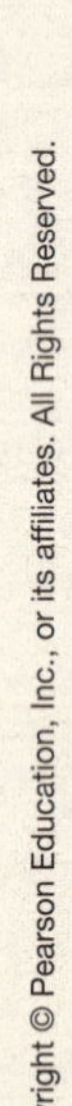

Name ______________________________

Explore the Text

Lesson 6

Lesson 7

Lesson 8

Children ask and answer questions about text to demonstrate comprehension.

Name ______________________________

Explore the Text

Lesson 9

Lesson 10

Children ask and answer questions about text to demonstrate comprehension.

Benchmark Vocabulary

Name ____________________

Lesson 6 wavers, bunched, bulging

Lesson 7 slick, trickles, sniffs

Children demonstrate contextual understanding of Benchmark Vocabulary.

Name ______________________________

Benchmark Vocabulary

Lesson 8 piled, dragged

Lesson 9 crunch, smacking

Lesson 10 heaping, handful, firm

Children demonstrate contextual understanding of Benchmark Vocabulary.

Name ___

Lesson 6 Listen to the words. Write the words.

Lesson 7 Write one of the sentences.

Lesson 8 Write the sentences.

Children practice various conventions of standard English.

Name ____________________

♥ Lesson 9 Write the sentences.

✱ Lesson 10 Write the sentences.

Children practice various conventions of standard English.

Name ____________________

Lesson 6 Draw a picture of the setting. Write about it.

Lesson 7 Write a detail about Mamma.

Lesson 8 Write your opinion. Write details that support it.

Children read text closely and use text evidence in their written answers.

Name ______________________

Writing in Response to Reading

♥ Lesson 9 Draw a picture of the setting. Write about it.

✱ Lesson 10 Write a list. Tell what Peter does.

Children read text closely and use text evidence in their written answers.

Rub the rug.

Rub, rub, rub.

Look! No milk.

What a Mess!

Look at the milk!

Did Rob spill the milk?

Did Russ spill the milk?

It is a mess!

Name ______________________

Run to get a mop.

Rob got a mop.

Mop up the milk fast.

Mop, mop, mop.

Is the rug wet?

Run to get a rag.

Russ got a rag.

Name ____________________

Name ______________________________

Lesson 11

Lesson 12

Children ask and answer questions about text to demonstrate comprehension.

Name ______________________

Explore the Text

Lesson 13

Children ask and answer questions about text to demonstrate comprehension.

Name ______________________________

Benchmark Vocabulary

Lesson 11 adventures, melted

Lesson 12 squinting, slick, crunch, heaping

Children demonstrate contextual understanding of Benchmark Vocabulary.

Name ____________________

Benchmark Vocabulary

☀ **Lesson 13** bunched, swollen, piled, firm

Children demonstrate contextual understanding of Benchmark Vocabulary.

Name ________________________

Conventions

Lesson 11 Listen to the words. Write the words.

Lesson 12 Write the sentences.

Children practice various conventions of standard English.

Name ______________________

Lesson 13 Circle the complete sentence.

Will and I

Will and I play.

Birds can fly.

Birds

Put the two parts together. Write the sentence.

The trip

was fun.

Write a complete sentence of your own.

Children practice various conventions of standard English.

Name ______________________

Lesson 11 Draw or write an answer to the question.

Lesson 12 Write your opinion. Write a detail that supports your opinion.

Lesson 13 Write about a character.

Children read text closely and use text evidence in their written answers.

Name ______________________________

Writing

Lesson 12 Draw pictures of the weather yesterday and today.

Children write routinely for a range of tasks, purposes, and audiences.

Did Dad fix it?

Yes, he did!

Kit is glad.

Dad Will Fix It

Kit has a doll.

See the dot on the doll.

Kit is sad.

Name ______________________

Dad will fix it.

He will dab the dot.

Dab the dot with a rag.

Look at the doll, Kit!

Do you see a dot?

We do not see a dot.

Name ______________________

Name ____________________

Explore the Text

● Lesson 1

■ Lesson 2

▲ Lesson 3

Children ask and answer questions about text to demonstrate comprehension.

Name ____________________

Explore the Text

Lesson 4

Lesson 5

Children ask and answer questions about text to demonstrate comprehension.

Name ______________________________

Benchmark Vocabulary

● **Lesson 1** sinking, puffy

■ **Lesson 2** forecast, predicting

▲ **Lesson 3** howl, wispy, drizzle

Children demonstrate contextual understanding of Benchmark Vocabulary.

Name ___________________________

Benchmark Vocabulary

Lesson 4 measure, temperature

Lesson 5 force, collapses

Children demonstrate contextual understanding of Benchmark Vocabulary.

Name ______________________

● Lesson 1 Write the words on the lines.

■ Lesson 2 Copy the sentence.

▲ Lesson 3

The book is <u>in the bag</u>.

The bird flies <u>out the window</u>.

We walk <u>to the park</u>.

She took a train <u>from New York</u>.

Children practice various conventions of standard English.

Name ______________________________

■ Lesson 4 Circle the prepositions. Underline the prepositional phrases.

The box is on the floor.

I read books for school.

The ball rolls off the table.

◆ Lesson 5 Circle the prepositions. Underline the prepositional phrases.

Mom opens the can of soup.

We drive by the store.

I dance with my doll.

Children practice various conventions of standard English.

Name ______________________________

● Lesson 1 Write your opinion.

■ Lesson 2 Write your opinion.

▲ Lesson 3 Draw a picture on a separate sheet of paper.
Write about your picture.

Children read text closely and use text evidence in their written answers.

Name ______________________________

Writing in Response to Reading

■ Lesson 4 Write your response.

◆ Lesson 5 Draw a picture. Write a sentence.

Children read text closely and use text evidence in their written answers.

Look at the fat figs.
Todd will sell them.
It is fun to sell stuff!

Let's Sell Stuff!

We are here to sell stuff.
What do we have?

Name ______________________________

I have five caps.

I will sell four to Bud.

They have a big blue rug.

They do not like it.

They will sell the rug.

Name ___________________________

Name ______________________

Explore the Text

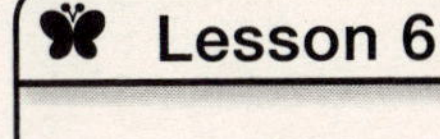
Lesson 6

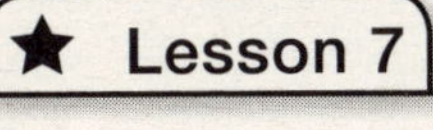
Lesson 7

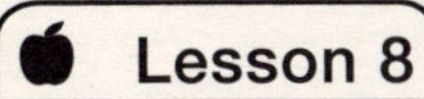
Lesson 8

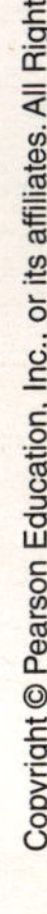

Children ask and answer questions about text to demonstrate comprehension.

Name ______________________________

Explore the Text

Lesson 9

Lesson 10

Children ask and answer questions about text to demonstrate comprehension.

Name ______________________________

Benchmark Vocabulary

Lesson 6 prepare

Lesson 7 fair, moisture, rises, sets, boundary

Lesson 8 position, evaporates, motion, freezes

Children demonstrate contextual understanding of Benchmark Vocabulary.

Name ____________________

Benchmark Vocabulary

Lesson 9 combinations, floods, expands, sunbeams

Lesson 10 direction, damage, twists

Children demonstrate contextual understanding of Benchmark Vocabulary.

Name ______________________

Conventions

Lesson 6 Listen to the words. Write the words on the lines.

Lesson 7 Copy the sentences.

Children practice various conventions of standard English.

Name ____________________

Conventions

Lesson 8 Copy the sentence. Add a detail.

The grass is green.

Lesson 9 Copy the sentence. Add an action.

The bird chirps.

Lesson 10 Copy the sentence. Add a noun to the subject.

The wind makes noise.

Children practice various conventions of standard English.

Name ______________________________

Lesson 6 Draw a picture of two antonyms and write the words.

Lesson 7 Draw a picture. Label it.

Children read text closely and use text evidence in their written answers.

Name ______________________________

Lesson 8 Write your response.

Lesson 9 Write your response.

Lesson 10 Write your opinion.

Children read text closely and use text evidence in their written answers.

Buzz! Buzz! Buzz!

Stop it! Stop it!

We fit the top on the box.

The Box

Where is the box?

We do not see the box.

Name ______________________________

Do you have the box?
Yes, I have the box!
Look in the box.
See the little doll.

Tick, tick, tick.
What is that?
Do you see a clock?
Yes, I see a red clock.

Name ______________________

Name ______________________________

Explore the Text

Lesson 11

Children ask and answer questions about text to demonstrate comprehension.

Name ______________________

Explore the Text

Lesson 12

Children ask and answer questions about text to demonstrate comprehension.

Name ______________________________

Lesson 11 predicting, sinking, fair, prepare

Children demonstrate contextual understanding of Benchmark Vocabulary.

Name ______________________________

Benchmark Vocabulary

Lesson 12 drizzle, collapses, boundary, damage

Children demonstrate contextual understanding of Benchmark Vocabulary.

Name ______________________

Lesson 11 Listen to the words. Write the words on the lines.

Children practice various conventions of standard English.

Name ______________________

Conventions

Lesson 12 Copy the sentences.

Children practice various conventions of standard English.

Name ______________________________

Lesson 11 Write your response.

Lesson 12 Write your response.

Children read text closely and use text evidence in their written answers.

Name ____________________

Writing

Lesson 11 Draw the main topic. Add details.

Write a sentence.

Children read text closely and use text evidence in their written answers.

But do not sob.

We can do lots.

We can run and hop and jump.

Here we go!

Lots to Do

What is it?

It is a little yellow bud.

Name ______________________________

We can cut the bud.
Stop! Do not cut the bud.
Dad will not like that.

What is it?
It is a big green bug.
Stop! Mom said stop!
Do not pat the bug.

Name ______________________________

Name ______________________

Explore the Text

● Lesson 1

■ Lesson 2

▲ Lesson 3

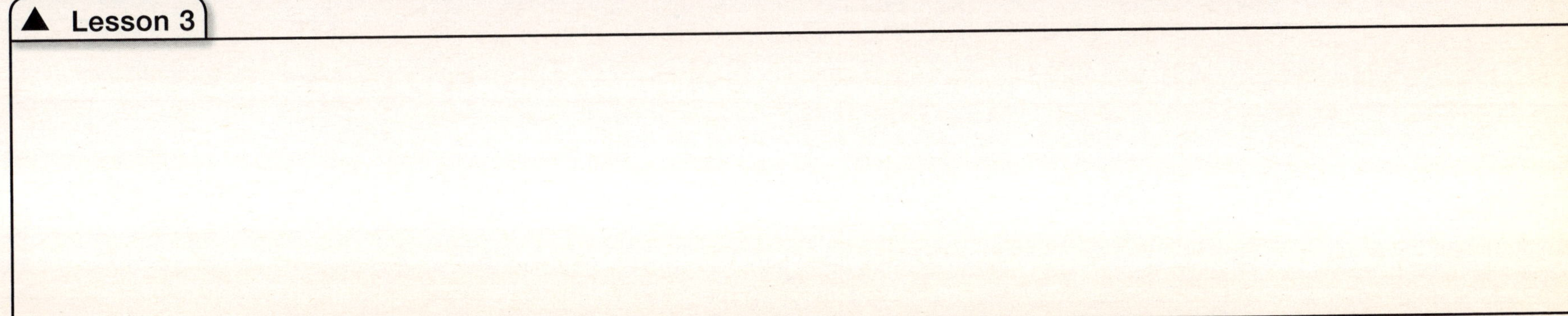

Children ask and answer questions about text to demonstrate comprehension.

Name ______________________________

Explore the Text

Lesson 4

Lesson 5

Children ask and answer questions about text to demonstrate comprehension.

Benchmark Vocabulary

Name ______________________________

● **Lesson 1** nibbling

■ **Lesson 2** sweetheart, darling

▲ **Lesson 3** spongy, honey

Children demonstrate contextual understanding of Benchmark Vocabulary.

Name ______________________________

Benchmark Vocabulary

Lesson 4 owls, collection, circus

Lesson 5 aquarium, seashore, pier, soars

Children demonstrate contextual understanding of Benchmark Vocabulary.

Name ______________________

● Lesson 1 Write the words.

■ Lesson 2 Write the sentence.

▲ Lesson 3 Circle the nouns.

jump pig home learn desk sister

Children practice various conventions of standard English.

Name ______________________________

■ Lesson 4 Draw a noun. Write a sentence.

◆ Lesson 5 Draw a noun. Write a sentence.

Children practice various conventions of standard English.

Name ______________________________

Lesson 1 Write how the experiences are the same or different.

Lesson 2 Write your opinion.

Children read text closely and use text evidence in their written answers.

Name ______________________________

Writing in Response to Reading

▲ Lesson 3 Write about the event.

▬ Lesson 4 Write about a character.

◆ Lesson 5 Write about your picture.

Children read text closely and use text evidence in their written answers.

The hat has got to go!

Hal likes his hat a lot.

But the hat is not for the hot sun.

Hal and His Hat

Hal has a hat.

He likes his hat a lot.

Name ______________________________

The hat has a big brim.

It has a big top too.

Hal sits in the sun in his hat.

The sun is hot.

The hat is hot.

Hal is HOT!

Name ______________________________

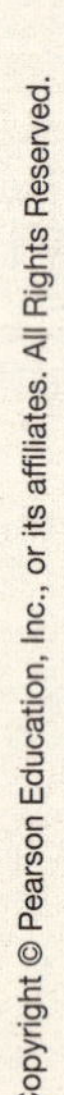

Name ______________________________

Lesson 6

Lesson 7

Lesson 8

Children ask and answer questions about text to demonstrate comprehension.

Name ____________________

Explore the Text

Lesson 9

Lesson 10

Children ask and answer questions about text to demonstrate comprehension.

Name ______________________

Benchmark Vocabulary

Lesson 6 trail, proud

Lesson 7 dollhouse

Lesson 8 cousins, traditional

Children demonstrate contextual understanding of Benchmark Vocabulary.

Name ________________________________

Benchmark Vocabulary

♥ **Lesson 9** fireworks, customers

✱ **Lesson 10** sample, few, straighten, videos

Children demonstrate contextual understanding of Benchmark Vocabulary.

Name ____________________

Lesson 6 Write the words.

Lesson 7 Write the sentences.

Children practice various conventions of standard English.

Name ______________________________

Conventions

Lesson 8 Circle the verbs.

tree sing fly leaf

Lesson 9 Circle the verbs.

draw ant boy eat

Lesson 10 Circle the verbs.

fox hike jog sun

Children practice various conventions of standard English.

Name ______________________________

Lesson 6 Write a sentence.

Lesson 7 Write about the gifts.

Children read text closely and use text evidence in their written answers.

Writing in Response to Reading

Name ______________________________

Lesson 8 Write your opinion.

Lesson 9 Write your response.

Lesson 10 Write a detail.

Children read text closely and use text evidence in their written answers.

Luck is a yellow Lab.

Lil will go home.

She will let Luck come in.

The List

Lil likes lists.

She jots jobs to do.

Name ______________________

Look at this list.

1. Fix lamp.
2. Let Luck in.

The lamp fell.

Lil will get it fixed.

Name ______________________________

Name ______________________

Explore the Text

Lesson 11

Lesson 12

Children ask and answer questions about text to demonstrate comprehension.

Name ______________________________________

Explore the Text

Lesson 13

Children ask and answer questions about text to demonstrate comprehension.

Name ______________________________

Benchmark Vocabulary

Lesson 11 rooftop, crowd, show

Lesson 12 aquarium, traditional, fireworks, customers

Children demonstrate contextual understanding of Benchmark Vocabulary.

Name ________________________________

Benchmark Vocabulary

Lesson 13 collection, spongy, straighten, few

Children demonstrate contextual understanding of Benchmark Vocabulary.

Name ______________________________

Lesson 11 Write the words.

Lesson 12 Write the sentences.

Children practice various conventions of standard English.

Name ______________________

Conventions

Lesson 13 Write *I* on the lines.

______ watch the game.

On Monday, ______ go to school.

Write a sentence.

____

Children practice various conventions of standard English.

Name ______________________________

Lesson 11 Write to tell what happens.

Lesson 12 Write your opinion.

Lesson 13 Write to tell what happens.

Children read text closely and use text evidence in their written answers.

Name ______________________

Writing

Lesson 13 Tell how they are alike.

Tell how they are different.

Children write routinely for a range of tasks, purposes, and audiences.

Then Mom comes.

She says, “Wait! Do drums and plants go in bags?”

Packing for a Trip

Brad and Fran have a bag.

They need to pack.

Name ______________________________

Brad packs his pants.

He adds his truck and his drum!

Fran packs her dress.

She adds her doll and her plant!

Name ______________________________

Name ____________________

Explore the Text

Lesson 1

Lesson 2

Lesson 3

Children ask and answer questions about text to demonstrate comprehension.

Name ______________________________

Explore the Text

Lesson 4

Lesson 5

Children ask and answer questions about text to demonstrate comprehension.

Name ______________________________

Benchmark Vocabulary

● **Lesson 1** land, nations

■ **Lesson 2** world

▲ **Lesson 3** celebrated, dish

Children demonstrate contextual understanding of Benchmark Vocabulary.

Name ______________________________

Benchmark Vocabulary

Lesson 4 overloaded

Lesson 5 past, present

Children demonstrate contextual understanding of Benchmark Vocabulary.

Name ______________________

Conventions

● Lesson 1 Write the words.

■ Lesson 2 Write the sentence.

▲ Lesson 3 Write your own complete sentence.

Children practice various conventions of standard English.

Name ____________________

Lesson 4 Write your own complete sentence.

Lesson 5 Copy the sentence. Add one or more words to the sentence.

We ate foods.

Children practice various conventions of standard English.

Name ______________________________

● Lesson 1 Write your opinion. Write a detail that supports it.

■ Lesson 2 Write your opinion. Write a detail that supports it.

Children read text closely and use text evidence in their written answers.

Name ______________________________

Writing in Response to Reading

▲ Lesson 3 Write your answer to the question.

▬ Lesson 4 Write your answer to the question.

◆ Lesson 5 Write your answer to the question.

Children read text closely and use text evidence in their written answers.

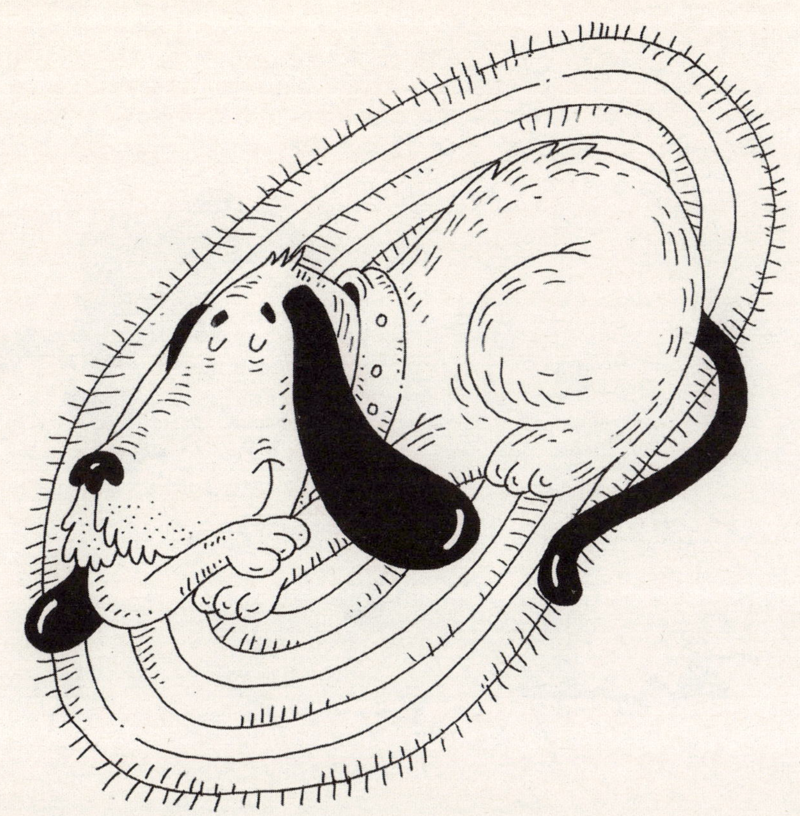

Gus is not a kid.

Gus is a dog.

We can get Gus a rug.

A Gift for Gus

Gus will be six.

What gift can we get for Gus?

Name ______________________________

Gus likes to tug on rags.
He likes to drag sticks.
He likes to dig up plants.

Rags? Sticks? Plants?
They are not gifts for
a kid.

Name ______________________

Name ______________________________

Explore the Text

Lesson 6

Lesson 7

Lesson 8

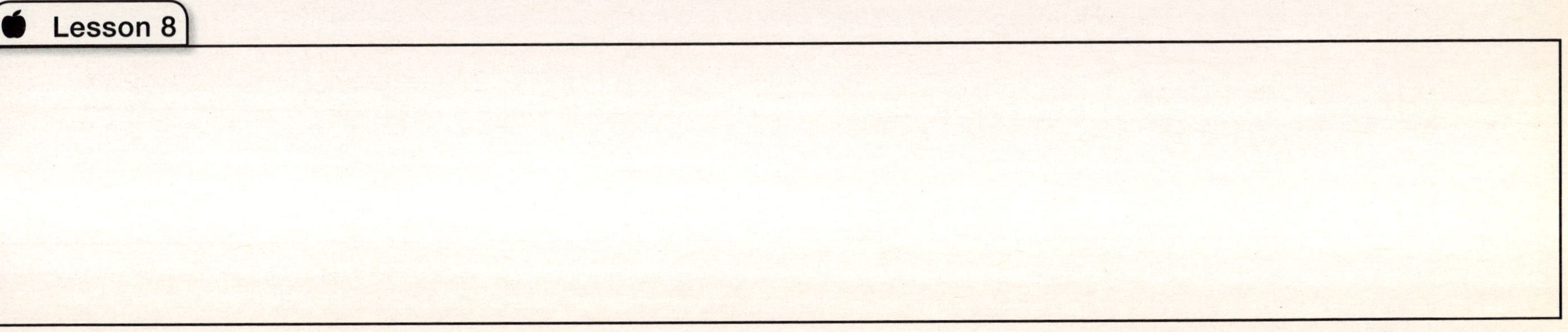

Children ask and answer questions about text to demonstrate comprehension.

Name ______________________________

Explore the Text

♥ Lesson 9

✱ Lesson 10

Children ask and answer questions about text to demonstrate comprehension.

Name ______________________________

Benchmark Vocabulary

Lesson 6 cultures, immigrants

Lesson 7 powwows, ceremonies

Lesson 8 parkas, sarongs

Children demonstrate contextual understanding of Benchmark Vocabulary.

Name ______________________________

Benchmark Vocabulary

♥ **Lesson 9** business suits, sturdy

✻ **Lesson 10** brides, grooms, kilts

Children demonstrate contextual understanding of Benchmark Vocabulary.

Name ______________________

Lesson 6 Write the words.

Lesson 7 Write the sentence.

Lesson 8 Write a sentence. Use the word *I*.

Children practice various conventions of standard English.

Name ______________________________

Conventions

♥ Lesson 9 Write the sentence. Add end punctuation.

✱ Lesson 10 Write the sentence. Add end punctuation.

Children practice various conventions of standard English.

Name ______________________________

Lesson 6 Write your answer to the question.

Lesson 7 Write your opinion and a detail.

Lesson 8 Write a detail about a photo.

Children read text closely and use text evidence in their written answers.

Name ______________________________

Writing in Response to Reading

Lesson 9 Write your opinion and a detail.

Lesson 10 Write to compare or contrast two kinds of clothes.

Children read text closely and use text evidence in their written answers.

Ned and Jen like the eggs.
"They are the best eggs!"

The Best Eggs

Deb has ten pet hens.
They lay many eggs.

Name ______________________

Deb tends to the hens.

Jess helps her.

They get eggs from the nests.

They sell the eggs.

Ned gets five.

Jen gets the rest.

Name ______________________________

Name ________________________________

Explore the Text

Lesson 11

Children ask and answer questions about text to demonstrate comprehension.

Name ______________________________

Explore the Text

Lesson 12

Children ask and answer questions about text to demonstrate comprehension.

Name ______________________________

Benchmark Vocabulary

Lesson 11 cultures, immigrants, parkas, sarongs

Children demonstrate contextual understanding of Benchmark Vocabulary.

Name ______________________________

Benchmark Vocabulary

Lesson 12 nations, celebrated, ceremonies, sturdy

Children demonstrate contextual understanding of Benchmark Vocabulary.

Name ______________________

Lesson 11 Write the words.

Write a sentence. Use *hen, pin,* or *sob.*

Children practice various conventions of standard English.

Name ______________________

Lesson 12 Write the sentences.

Write two sentences of your own.

Children practice various conventions of standard English.

Name ______________________

Writing in Response to Reading

Lesson 11 Write about a detail from one text.

Lesson 12 Write your opinion and a detail.

Children read text closely and use text evidence in their written answers.

Name ________________________________

Writing

Lesson 11 Draw or write how the books are alike.
Draw or write how the books are different.

Alike	Different

Children write routinely for a range of tasks, purposes, and audiences.

"I will help you, Jeff."
Bess helped Jeff, and
Jeff did well on the test.

Jeff and the Test

Jeff sits at his desk.
He has a test to take.
But Jeff is not well.

Name ______________________

His mom sends him to bed.

"No test for you.

You have to rest."

Jeff missed the test.

Bess comes to see Jeff.

Name ____________________

Name ______________________________

Explore the Text

● **Lesson 1**

■ **Lesson 2**

▲ **Lesson 3**

Children ask and answer questions about text to demonstrate comprehension.

Name ______________________________

Explore the Text

▬ Lesson 4

◆ Lesson 5

Children ask and answer questions about text to demonstrate comprehension.

Name ______________________________

Lesson 1 sails, tiny

Lesson 2 strong, rays

Children demonstrate contextual understanding of Benchmark Vocabulary.

Name ___________________________________

Benchmark Vocabulary

▲ **Lesson 3** drifts, pushes

▬ **Lesson 4** settle

◆ **Lesson 5** burst

Children demonstrate contextual understanding of Benchmark Vocabulary.

Name ______________________

● Lesson 1 Write the words.

■ Lesson 2 Write the sentence.

▲ Lesson 3 Write one of your questions. Underline the question word.

Children practice various conventions of standard English.

Name ______________________

Conventions

Lesson 4 Write one of your questions. Underline the question word.

Lesson 5 Write the sentence.

Write your own sentence with the word *I*.

Children practice various conventions of standard English.

Name ______________________

● Lesson 1 Write your opinion. Write a detail that supports it.

■ Lesson 2 Write your opinion. Write a detail that supports it.

Children read text closely and use text evidence in their written answers.

Name

Writing in Response to Reading

▲ Lesson 3 Write your answer to the question.

▬ Lesson 4 Write the word. Write its meaning.

◆ Lesson 5 Rewrite a sentence in your own words.

Children read text closely and use text evidence in their written answers.

Jill and Wes get to the line at the same time!

Jill *and* Wes win the race!

Jill and Wes Race

Jill and Wes will run in a race.

They both think, "I want to win."

Name ______________________________

It is time for the race.
Line up, get set, go!

Who will win?
Jill runs like the wind.
Wes runs like a jet.

Name ______________________________

Name ___________________________________

Explore the Text

Lesson 6

Lesson 7

Lesson 8

Children ask and answer questions about text to demonstrate comprehension.

Name ________________

♥ Lesson 9

✱ Lesson 10

Children ask and answer questions about text to demonstrate comprehension.

Name ______________________

Benchmark Vocabulary

Lesson 6 far, near

Lesson 7 shakes

Children demonstrate contextual understanding of Benchmark Vocabulary.

Name ______________________________

Benchmark Vocabulary

Lesson 8 garden

Lesson 9 planted

✱ Lesson 10 blossomed

Children demonstrate contextual understanding of Benchmark Vocabulary.

Name

Conventions

Lesson 6 Write the words.

Lesson 7 Write the sentence.

Lesson 8 Write your sentence.

Children practice various conventions of standard English.

Name ______________________

♥ Lesson 9 Write your sentence.

✱ Lesson 10 Write your question.

Children practice various conventions of standard English.

Name ______________________

Writing in Response to Reading

Lesson 6 Write your opinion. Write a detail that supports it.

Lesson 7 Write your sentence.

Children read text closely and use text evidence in their written answers.

Name ______

Writing in Response to Reading

Lesson 8 Write a detail about the garden.

Lesson 9 Write your answer to the question.

✱ Lesson 10 Write your answer to the question.

Children read text closely and use text evidence in their written answers.

Thump! Thump! Crack!

Max sets the box on
the rug.

This is a good time to go.

Max and the Box

Max sees a big box.

He wants to look in it.

Dad calls, "Not
yet, Max!"

Name ______________________

Max sits next to the box.
What is in this box?

Max picks up the box.
He shakes it just a little.

Name ______________________

Name ________________________________

Explore the Text

Lesson 11

Lesson 12

Children ask and answer questions about text to demonstrate comprehension.

Name ______________________________

Explore the Text

Lesson 13

Children ask and answer questions about text to demonstrate comprehension.

Name ______________________________

Benchmark Vocabulary

Lesson 11 sipped, chased

Lesson 12 strong, drifts, planted, blossomed

Children demonstrate contextual understanding of Benchmark Vocabulary.

Name ______________________________

Benchmark Vocabulary

☀ Lesson 13 settle, burst, sipped, chased

Children demonstrate contextual understanding of Benchmark Vocabulary.

Name

Conventions

Lesson 11 Write your exclamation.

Lesson 12 Write the words.

Children practice various conventions of standard English.

Name ______________________

Lesson 13 Write the sentence.

Write your own sentence.

Children practice various conventions of standard English.

Name ______________________

Writing in Response to Reading

Lesson 11 Write a sentence using the word you chose.

Lesson 12 Write your opinion.

Lesson 13 Write your opinion.

Children read text closely and use text evidence in their written answers.

Name ______________________________

Writing in Response to Reading

Lesson 12 Draw or write the answers to the questions.

Similar	**Different**

Write your opinion.

Children write routinely for a range of tasks, purposes, and audiences.

At last we get rid of that bad smell!

Or did we?

Sniff, sniff. Ewwwww!

Ruff and the Skunk

Ruff chases a skunk.

The skunk makes Ruff smell bad!

Name ______________________________

Ruff rubs on the rug.
Do not do that, Ruff!
You will get the smell
on the rug.

We get Ruff into the tub.
We rub and scrub him.
We scrub and rub him.

Name ______________________

Name ______________________________

Explore the Text

● Lesson 1

■ Lesson 2

▲ Lesson 3

Children ask and answer questions about text to demonstrate comprehension.

Name ______________________________

Explore the Text

Lesson 4

Lesson 5

Children ask and answer questions about text to demonstrate comprehension.

Name ______________________________

Benchmark Vocabulary

● **Lesson 1** pattern, repeated

■ **Lesson 2** trimmed, form

▲ **Lesson 3** single

Children demonstrate contextual understanding of Benchmark Vocabulary.

Name ______________________________

Benchmark Vocabulary

Lesson 4 circles, stalk

Lesson 5 scatter, petals, center

Children demonstrate contextual understanding of Benchmark Vocabulary.

Name

● Lesson 1 Write the words.

■ Lesson 2 Copy the sentence.

▲ Lesson 3 Write the nouns for more than one.

Children practice various conventions of standard English.

Name ______________________

Conventions

Lesson 4 Write the nouns for more than one.

Lesson 5 Write the nouns for more than one.

Children practice various conventions of standard English.

Name ______________________

Writing in Response to Reading

● Lesson 1 Write about a plant pattern.

■ Lesson 2 Write your response.

▲ Lesson 3 Write about your picture.

Children read text closely and use text evidence in their written answers.

Name ______________________

Writing in Response to Reading

Lesson 4 Write your opinion. Tell why.

Lesson 5 Draw a picture.

Label your picture with the word.

Children read text closely and use text evidence in their written answers.

Gus said, "Come on, Buck.
The ducks do not want us here.
This is their tub."

I Can Read Reader 28

Ducks in a Tub

"Rub-a-dub, dub, three ducks in a tub."
In fact, the tub was a big pond.

Name ______________________

The ducks looked for bugs to eat.
Then Gus's pup ran to the pond.

"Ruff, ruff!" the pup said.
The ducks swam from Gus and the pup.

Name ______________________________

Name ______________________________

Explore the Text

Lesson 6

Lesson 7

Lesson 8

Children ask and answer questions about text to demonstrate comprehension.

Name ______________________

Explore the Text

♥ Lesson 9

✱ Lesson 10

Children ask and answer questions about text to demonstrate comprehension.

Name ___________________________

Lesson 6 scroll, fiddle, alternate

Lesson 7 tropical, hollow

Lesson 8 spiral, drought, swirl

Children demonstrate contextual understanding of Benchmark Vocabulary.

Name ____________________

Benchmark Vocabulary

♥ **Lesson 9** coiled, curves

✱ **Lesson 10** winds, clever, stretches

Children demonstrate contextual understanding of Benchmark Vocabulary.

Name ______________________

Lesson 6 Write the words.

Lesson 7 Copy the sentence.

Lesson 8 Circle the verb for now.

She (tell tells) a story.

I (calls call) my mom.

We (makes make) a loud noise.

Children practice various conventions of standard English.

Name ______________________

Conventions

♥ Lesson 9 Circle the verb for the past.

She (wanted wants) a toy.

I (need needed) my mom.

We (called call) our aunt.

✱ Lesson 10 Complete the sentence.

She ______________ read a book.

They ______________ see you later.

Children practice various conventions of standard English.

Name ______________________________

Lesson 6 Write the answer to the question.

Lesson 7 Write your response.

Children read text closely and use text evidence in their written answers.

Name ______________________________

Writing in Response to Reading

Lesson 8 Draw a picture. Write about it.

Lesson 9 Write your opinion.

✱ Lesson 10 Write the word in a sentence.

Children read text closely and use text evidence in their written answers.

At home Zip wants to zig and zag.

It is good to have Zip back.

Zig and Zag

Zip zigs this way.

Zip zags that way.

Viv smiles.

Name ________________________

Then Zip gets sick.

He will not zig and zag.

Mom and Viv take Zip to the vet.

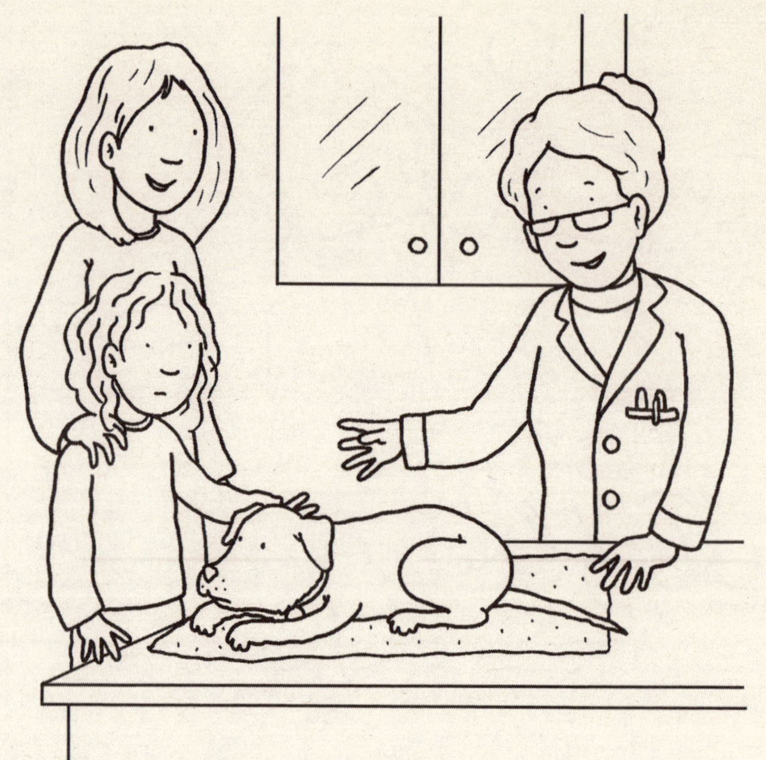

"Can you help him?" Viv asks.

Bev the vet helps Zip get well.

Name ______________________________

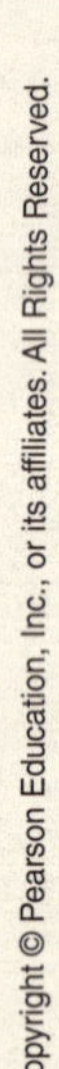

Name ______________________________

Explore the Text

Lesson 11

Children ask and answer questions about text to demonstrate comprehension.

Name ______________________________

Explore the Text

Lesson 12

Children ask and answer questions about text to demonstrate comprehension.

Name ______________________________

Benchmark Vocabulary

Lesson 11 pattern, stalk, swirl, curves

Children demonstrate contextual understanding of Benchmark Vocabulary.

Name ______________________________

Benchmark Vocabulary

Lesson 12 scatter, fiddle, winds, stretches

Children demonstrate contextual understanding of Benchmark Vocabulary.

Name ___________________________

Lesson 11 Write the words.

Write a sentence. Use *brim, drum*, or *stop*.

Children practice various conventions of standard English.

Name ______________________

Conventions

Lesson 12 Write the sentences.

Write two sentences of your own.

Children practice various conventions of standard English.

Name

Lesson 11 Write your opinion.

Lesson 12 Write a detail.

Children read text closely and use text evidence in their written answers.

Name ____________________

Writing

Lesson 11 Draw the pattern. Write about it.

Children write routinely for a range of tasks, purposes, and audiences.

It was quite a task, but they did it.

The duck quacked as it swam off.

Quinn and Dad Help

Quinn and Dad were looking at the ducks.

Quinn saw one small duck.

Name ______________________

"Dad!" yelled Quinn.
"Look at that duck!"

They saw one leg was
stuck in the twigs.

"Quick," said Dad,
"I will grasp the duck.

You yank the twigs."

Name ______________________

Name ____________________

Explore the Text

● Lesson 1

■ Lesson 2

▲ Lesson 3

Children ask and answer questions about text to demonstrate comprehension.

Name ______________________

Explore the Text

Lesson 4

Lesson 5

Children ask and answer questions about text to demonstrate comprehension.

Name ______________________________

Benchmark Vocabulary

● **Lesson 1** explore

■ **Lesson 2** speckled, notebook

▲ **Lesson 3** handsome

Children demonstrate contextual understanding of Benchmark Vocabulary.

Name ___________________________________

Benchmark Vocabulary

Lesson 4 genius, writing, bingo

Lesson 5 whiz, polishing

Children demonstrate contextual understanding of Benchmark Vocabulary.

Name

● Lesson 1 Write the words.

■ Lesson 2 Write the sentence.

▲ Lesson 3 Write a complete sentence.

Children practice various conventions of standard English.

Name ______________________

Conventions

Lesson 4 Add a punctuation mark.

Look out ____

What time is it ____

He walks to the store ____

Lesson 5 Write a sentence. Add a punctuation mark.

Children practice various conventions of standard English.

Name ______________________

● Lesson 1 Write your response.

■ Lesson 2 Write your opinion.

▲ Lesson 3 Write your response.

Children read text closely and use text evidence in their written answers.

Name

Writing in Response to Reading

Lesson 4 Write your opinion.

Lesson 5 Write a sentence.

Children read text closely and use text evidence in their written answers.

Brad rakes up leaves.

He stuffs them into bags.

What are the next tasks on the list?

The Task List

The Hills have tasks to do.

They look at the list.

Name ______________________

Kim makes the bed with fresh sheets.

Rick mops the tiles and scrubs the tub.

Gram sets the plants in the sun.

Dad hangs the mats.

Name ______________________________

Name ______________________

Explore the Text

Lesson 6

Lesson 7

Lesson 8

Children ask and answer questions about text to demonstrate comprehension.

Name ______________________

Explore the Text

♥ Lesson 9

✱ Lesson 10

Children ask and answer questions about text to demonstrate comprehension.

Name ______________________________

Benchmark Vocabulary

Lesson 6 sweetly

Lesson 7 listening, porch

Lesson 8 apartment

Children demonstrate contextual understanding of Benchmark Vocabulary.

Name ______________________________

Benchmark Vocabulary

♥ **Lesson 9** lined

✱ **Lesson 10** rush, strangers, bandage

Children demonstrate contextual understanding of Benchmark Vocabulary.

Name ______________________

Lesson 6 Write the words.

Lesson 7 Write the sentence.

Lesson 8 Copy the sentence. Add one or more words.

I go outside.

Children practice various conventions of standard English.

Name ______________________

♥ Lesson 9 Copy the sentence. Add one or more words.

We see places.

✱ Lesson 10 Add end punctuation.

Can we go ____

Let's go fast ____

My home is nice ____

Children practice various conventions of standard English.

Name ______________________________

Lesson 6 Draw a picture. Label your picture.

Lesson 7 Write your opinion.

Children read text closely and use text evidence in their written answers.

Name

Writing in Response to Reading

Lesson 8 Write your answer.

Lesson 9 Write your answer.

Lesson 10 Write your answer.

Children read text closely and use text evidence in their written answers.

Bob hops up and gets a spot.

Bob can sit in the hot sun with Ron.

On a Log in a Bog

Ron the snake sits on a log in a bog.

The log is in the sun.

Name ______________________

Ron is thin and has spots and dots.

Hop, hop! Here comes Bob the frog.

"You will not bite me, will you, Ron?"

"I will not bite you, Bob."

Name ______________________________

Name ____________________

Explore the Text

Lesson 11

Lesson 12

Children ask and answer questions about text to demonstrate comprehension.

Name ______________________________

Explore the Text

Lesson 13

Children ask and answer questions about text to demonstrate comprehension.

Name ______________________

Benchmark Vocabulary

Lesson 11 checks out

Lesson 12 explore, genius, lined, rush

Children demonstrate contextual understanding of Benchmark Vocabulary.

Name ______________________________

Benchmark Vocabulary

Lesson 13 polishing, listening, strangers, bandage

Children demonstrate contextual understanding of Benchmark Vocabulary.

Name

Lesson 11 Write the words.

Lesson 12 Write the sentences.

Children practice various conventions of standard English.

Name ______________________________

Lesson 13 Write the sentences.

when can i come?

my dog and i play.

Write your own sentence.

Children practice various conventions of standard English.

Name ______________________

Lesson 11 Write your answer.

Lesson 12 Write your opinion.

Lesson 13 Write your answer.

Children read text closely and use text evidence in their written answers.

Name ______________________

Writing

Lesson 13 Write about your community.

Write your opinion.

Children write routinely for a range of tasks, purposes, and audiences.

What if we went for a nice run, first?

Ben yelps yes!

Ben Begs

This is my dog Ben.

Look at Ben beg!

Name ______________________

What does Ben want?

Does he want beets?

Does he want eggs and ham?

Ben does not want beets, eggs, or ham.

Ben wants a bone.

Name ______________________

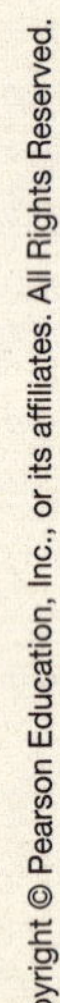

Name ______________________________

Explore the Text

● Lesson 1

■ Lesson 2

▲ Lesson 3

Children ask and answer questions about text to demonstrate comprehension.

Name ______________________________

Explore the Text

■ Lesson 4

◆ Lesson 5

Children ask and answer questions about text to demonstrate comprehension.

Name ______________________________

Benchmark Vocabulary

● Lesson 1 metropolitan

■ Lesson 2 thousands, millions, crowded

Children demonstrate contextual understanding of Benchmark Vocabulary.

Name ___________________________________

Benchmark Vocabulary

▲ **Lesson 3** repair, workers

▬ **Lesson 4** products, grouped

◆ **Lesson 5** borrow, offer

Children demonstrate contextual understanding of Benchmark Vocabulary.

Name ______________________

● Lesson 1 Write the words.

■ Lesson 2 Write the sentence.

▲ Lesson 3 Write the words. Add *-s* or *-es*.

job

box

Children practice various conventions of standard English.

Name ______________________

Conventions

Lesson 4 Write the words. Add *-s* or *-es*.

car

bus

Lesson 5 Write your sentence. Use a noun and a verb.

Children practice various conventions of standard English.

Name ______________________________

● Lesson 1 Write about one part of a city.

■ Lesson 2 Write your connection.

Children read text closely and use text evidence in their written answers.

Name ______________________

Writing in Response to Reading

▲ Lesson 3 Write the word. Write its meaning.

▬ Lesson 4 Write your opinion.

◆ Lesson 5 Write your idea.

Children read text closely and use text evidence in their written answers.

"Too many bumps for me.
Next time I will ride the bus."

The Truck Ride

Bump! Thump! Bump!
Bud said, "This is *not* fun!
I do not like this truck."

Name ______________________

"Do not fuss," said Huck.
"There are many bumps.
But I think this *is* fun!"

Bump! Thump! BAM!
Bud drops his mug and his hot drink spills on the floor.

Name ______________________________

Name ______________________________

Lesson 6

Lesson 7

Lesson 8

Children ask and answer questions about text to demonstrate comprehension.

Name ___________________________

Explore the Text

♥ Lesson 9

✱ Lesson 10

Children ask and answer questions about text to demonstrate comprehension.

Name ___________________________________

Benchmark Vocabulary

Lesson 6 leaders, fancy

Lesson 7 collect

Lesson 8 messenger, delivery, shortcuts

Children demonstrate contextual understanding of Benchmark Vocabulary.

Name ______________________________

Benchmark Vocabulary

♥ **Lesson 9** groove, zips, skitters

✱ **Lesson 10** squints, blare, sirens, flickering

Children demonstrate contextual understanding of Benchmark Vocabulary.

Name ______________________

Lesson 6 Write the words.

Lesson 7 Write the sentence.

Lesson 8 Copy the sentence. Add one or more words.

He has a bike.

Children practice various conventions of standard English.

Name ______________________

Conventions

Lesson 9 Copy the sentence. Add one or more words.

He crosses a bridge.

Lesson 10 Copy the sentence. Add one or more words.

He rides home.

Children practice various conventions of standard English.

Name ______________________________

Lesson 6 Write your opinion. Write a detail that supports it.

Lesson 7 Write your ideas.

Children read text closely and use text evidence in their written answers.

Name ______________________

Writing in Response to Reading

Lesson 8 Write your answer to the question.

Lesson 9 Write your answer to the question.

Lesson 10 Write your opinion. Write a detail that supports it.

Children read text closely and use text evidence in their written answers.

The gifts will make Mom smile and Dad grin.

The kids think the gifts look good!

The Kids Make Gifts

The kids want to make gifts for Mom and Dad.

Name ______________________

Ann makes a mask from a plate.

It looks like a cat.

The mask is for Mom.

Jed makes a vest from green felt.

The vest is for Dad.

Name ______________________

Name ______________________

Lesson 11

Children ask and answer questions about text to demonstrate comprehension.

Name ______________________________

Explore the Text

Lesson 12

Children ask and answer questions about text to demonstrate comprehension.

Name ______________________________

Benchmark Vocabulary

Lesson 11 metropolitan, repair, messenger, delivery

Children demonstrate contextual understanding of Benchmark Vocabulary.

Name ______________________________

Benchmark Vocabulary

Lesson 12 borrow, offer, squints, blare

Children demonstrate contextual understanding of Benchmark Vocabulary.

Name ______________________________

Lesson 11 Finish each sentence. Write the word *in*, *on*, or *to*.

Many people live ______________ apartments.

Some children walk ______________ school.

Calvin sits ______________ his bike.

Write your own sentence. Use the phrase *at night*.

____

____

Children practice various conventions of standard English.

Name ______________________

Conventions

Lesson 12 Finish each sentence. Write the word *by*, *from*, or *with*.

We can get books ______________ a library..

Calvin takes his bike ______________ him.

People hurry ______________ the store windows.

Write your own sentence. Use the phrase *in a city*.

Children practice various conventions of standard English.

Name ______________________

Lesson 11 Write your opinion. Write a detail that supports it.

Lesson 12 Write a way to find the answers.

Children read text closely and use text evidence in their written answers.

Name ______________________

Writing

Lesson 12 Draw or write your ideas.

Living in a City	
Advantages	**Disadvantages**

Draw or write your ideas.

Children write routinely for a range of tasks, purposes, and audiences.

The bus takes us home.

Dad asks, "Did you have fun?"

Yes! Can we go back?

Going to Camp

We are going to camp!

Look, here comes the bus.

Quick, get on.

Name ______________________________

What will we do at camp?

We will swim in the lake and sing songs at the fire.

We will sleep in tents.

We will hike and ride bikes.

The time will go fast.

Name ______________________________